SIXTY THINGS YOU MUST DO BEFORE AGE SIXTY

BY
BISHOP OCHEI INNOCENT.

Copyright reserved. No part of this book may be reproduced without the written permission of the author or publisher.

"The heads of strong old age are beautiful/Beyond all grace of youth"

— Robinson Jeffers

https://www.goodreads.com/quotes/tag/age

DEDICATION

To all between the ages of 18 and 60 years old. May these words help you in life and ministry!

And to those 70 years and above. I entreat you to believe in God of a second chance.

He will not let you down. He never does.

WHY THIS BOOK?

In 1975 when I was going out on my own, to earn a living for the first time in life, my father called me and told me five things that have helped me to deal with the challenges of life to some great levels.

The things he told me are worth more than gold and silver. They have helped open great doors unto me and kept many open to date.

His itemized words of advice so helped me that I now see the need to do the same for my children – that is, provide the benefit of my life's lessons to my children and their contemporaries.

It is three days to my sixty-first birth day. I asked myself some days ago, what legacies will I be leaving for the coming generation in addition to a good name, sound education and adequately defined and communicated family values?

As I pondered over this, I felt a leading to review my first sixty years on earth. What do I consider avoidable pitfalls and success? Now that God has permitted me to cross age sixty, what things do I feel a man should do before reaching age sixty?

I also considered that I have five more years to reach the mandatory retirement age of six-five in my country. So what are those things I know or have read that a person should do before age sixty-five?

I feel I have something to share because of the diversity of experience God has allowed me to acquire. He has allowed me to pass through fire and water, travel across several nations and cities, be born to a mixed family, and be lost in sin before being found by my Lord Jesus Christ.

I was born with a silver spoon but lost that proverbial eating tool to the civil war. My father was already a manager in Kaduna before the civil war started. We became internally displaced by the war and that threw the silver spoon out of my mouth. I had to fend for myself from high school upwards. Money was borrowed to pay my secondary school fees up to high school form five and for me to sit the qualifying exams.

I had also to go and work as an auxiliary teacher for a year before proceeding to the Hospital Management of Board of the then Bendel State of Nigeria as a Medical Records Administrator having attended a crash course for six months both at the Specialist Hospital and the in Benin City.

I moved to Lagos thereafter and taught also in a private secondary school for nine months before proceeding to Federal Polytechnic, Ilaro where I later became the first elected public relations officer of the student's government.

From there I began to do a lot of private studies and ended up as a newsmagazine editor. Later I worked with Zoe Ministries World-wide which as at 1992 had over a thousand branches.

On the whole, I have lived without parental control for over forty years.

This book enables me share essential truths I have picked up in life and which should help anybody who cares to read it to the end.

"There is a fountain of youth: it is your mind, your talents, the creativity you bring to your life and the lives of people you love. When you learn to tap this source, you will truly have defeated age."

— Sophia Loren

CULLED FROM:
https://www.goodreads.com/quotes/tag/age

SIXTY THINGS

YOU MUST DO BEFORE AGE SIXTY

"Growing old is mandatory; growing up is optional."

- *Chili Davis*

CULLED FROM: http://www.flokka.com/60th-birthday-quotes/

LESSON NUMBER ONE

ACCEPT JESUS CHRIST EARLY.

Because the spiritual controls the physical, I would like to start by urging you to give your life to Jesus Christ if you have not already done so.
Unless a man accepts Jesus Christ as his or personal Lord and Savior, his life will be full of crisis.

Please, if in doubt, ask those who were formally in sin but have repented. Look at their life style today and you will see evidence of what Jesus Christ can do in your life because he alone is the answer to all the question mankind has.

LESSON NUMBER TWO

ASK FOR THE HOLY GHOST IMMEDIATELY.

After giving your life to Jesus Christ, ask for the Holy Spirit.

He is the Teacher and Comforter given to us to direct and guide us through these turbulent times.

When you have Holy Spirit in your life, he enables you do exploits.

LESSON NUMBER THREE

LEARN TO PRAY

When we pray, God answers. When we pray, we get God involved in what we are doing.

When we fail to pray, we do things on our own. Prayers is the key to everything we do or want to do in life.

Why would a Christian not pray when we are promised that we should ask anything in the name of Jesus Christ and it will be done for us?

Praying shows how humble we are. The Bible says if the people which are called by my name shall humble themselves and call my name, I shall hear from heaven and heal their land.
Therefore, learn to pray without ceasing, if want to excel in life and ministry.

LESSON NUMBER FOUR

KNOW THE HISTORY OF YOUR FAMILY

Find out where your parents came from and how they reached where they are in life. Dig into their history. Dig well and deep. Find out about your ancestors. Their life styles and occupations.

Did they come under any curse? Did they fail to keep promises made? Did they live a life of mercy to others or sowed seeds of discord? Did they do anything you should apologize for and pay reparations if necessary?

Are there noticeable patterns in their life styles? Such as recurrent divorces and chronic illnesses? What about persistent social climbing difficulties and limitations or ceilings?

Knowing these things will help you pray better, having known what to expect and ambush. An apple does not fall far from the tree. Most curses are inherited. Doctors say diagnosis is fifty percent cure.

LESSON NUMBER FIVE

KNOW YOUR FAMILY VALUES

When we were growing up as young boys, our parents used to admonish us to always remember the sons and daughters of who we are. In other words, we should remember that our family would not accept certain types of conduct.

I specifically remember my grandfather on more than one occasion, telling me that I had no right picking up something valuable I found lying on the road since it was not mine. He said something found without an owner does not amount to a right for me to pick it up, knowing that it could not have fallen from the sky but must belong to somebody who misplaced it. So why not leave it there for the owner to come back and find?
Knowing your family value helps you stay in line all your life.

LESSON NUMBER SIX

DEVELOP YOUR PERSONAL VALUES

As you go to school and climb the social ladder, experiencing some of the things your parents and relations never experienced, chances are that you will develop more elevating values than they did.

Nothing helps us to think and act out of the box than formal education. The more educated we are the better we are in handling issues with less crisis.

As we go to school, we must allow the school to go through us and not end up with an empty head. As the years go by and moth has eaten up the certificates, what remains are the things that entered the brain and not the marks on the scroll.

LESSON NUMBER SEVEN

DEFINE YOUR NUCLEAR FAMILY SIZE

The Bible cautions us to do all things in moderation. Plan your family size early enough.

When God said go ye and multiply, I do not believe that he meant go ye and proliferate. Learn to cut your coat in moderation.

LESSON NUMBER EIGHT

KNOW YOUR BLOOD GROUP

Believe me, not until I had gone past fifty years that I began to probe my blood group. Some of us were born in hospitals where there were neither equipment not records.

That was a grave error because if I had gotten into an accident and needed blood in emergency, my life would have been endangered by my own negligence.

Some more fortunate ones are daily born in places with these facilities but with time, they lose their medical records. Please ensure that your record your blood group in as many places as possible.

LESSON NUMBER NINE

READ SIXTY NEW BOOKS EVERY YEAR

Though I do not agree with those who say that information is power, the truth remains that information is very important because it enhances power. Jesus Christ spent some three and a half years dishing out information to his disciples. Yet, before ascending, he said to them, do not venture into ministry just with information. You need to have the Holy Spirit who will teach you how to effectively use the information at your disposal.

Information enables us to use power wisely and to achieve better results than ignoramuses.

What we get when we read books is information and information when skillfully applied, is wisdom and in life, according to the Bible, is the principal thing.

LESSON NUMBER TEN

LEARN TO THINK STRATEGICALLY

Cease to live for the moment. Some folks never think of tomorrow. What informs their actions ad inactions, are nothing but thoughts of immediate gratification!

That is why for instance, they do not save for rainy days. Since they only have eyes for the harvest, they fail to see that the fruits contain seeds that need to be planted for future harvest. So they eat both the fruit and the seed.

Think and plan ahead. Know that the future will surely come whether you plan for it or not.

LESSON NUMBER ELEVEN

LEARN TO SET STRATEGIC GOALS

Now, you are able to work and earn a living. What happens when you are tired and too weak to work on account of age and stress? Learn to set goals that will assist you in the long run and not only the ones that pander to the needs of today.

If you are a senior pastor or founder, what are your plans for when you are no more furnishing a pulpit? Where will you live when you are seventy and above? Will there be stair cases or lifts in the building? What measures are you putting in place to ensure that where you live is old age friendly?

LESSON NUMBER TWELVE
LEARN TO STAY FOCUSED

Learn early to stay focused on goals set, no matter the distractions and odds. Life is full of distractions and diversions.

Africans love to tell the story of how man sent to God to pleading that man should no longer die. God is said to have agreed on one condition: that two beasts should be sent to intercede on behalf of man. Whatever, the first animal pleaded would be acceptable to God.

Man was very pleased with the request. He quickly sent the Dog to tell God that man should no longer die. As requested by God that two animals be sent with different messages, Tortoise was also sent but with the message that man should continue dying. Trust man: he thought that he had it all sealed since everyone in the world knew that while Dog was very fast, Tortoise was as slow as millipede.

Wishes are no horses however. Soon as the destiny changing race began, Dog perceived the sweet smelling aroma of a well prepared dish and left the track to go and investigate with the hope that there would be time enough to investigate and return to win the race. He got there, saw the dish and began to help himself. While he ate, he did not know that time was flying.

Meanwhile, the slow, steady and steel willed Tortoise crawled to the finishing line. He met God and delivered his message. He was on the way back when Dog with great speed dashed past on his way. When Dog got to God, he was shocked to hear that Tortoise had already been there.
He wept but it was already too late. And according to the great griots of Africa, that is why man still has to face death at one time or the other till date.

Take note therefore that only a man with determination, persistence and focus will reach where he is going.

"And in the end, it's not the years in your life that count. It's the life in your years."

Abraham Lincoln

CULLED FROM: http://www.flokka.com/60th-birthday-quotes/

LESSON NUMBER THIRTEEN
KNOW YOUR TIMES AND SEASONS

The Bible tells me that for everything under the sun, there is a time and season. A man must know his times and seasons.

There is a time to be a child and a time to be a man. At all times, we must know what is needful.

There is a time to be foolish and a time to be wise. There is a time to say yes to a man and a time to say no. an under aged girl cannot say yes to a suitor. She will do well to ask the suitor to allow her go to school or go ask her parents.
She should know when to decide for herself and when to seek parental counsel or go irredeemably astray in life.

LESSON NUMBER FOURTEEN

LEARN TO RESPOND. NOT REACT.

Learn to happen to things instead of allowing things to happen to you. Arrange things and not allow others to re-arrange you. Nothing happens by accident. Whatever is, are things we allow.

If we fail to sow, we fail to harvest. It is better to attack than to defend.

If you do not like the atmosphere, recreate it to suit your purpose. Be a change agent and not a complainant.

LESSON NUMBER FIFTEEN

LEARN TO SPEND OTHER PEOPLE'S MONEY

Partner with those who have money.

Come up with ideas that people cannot ignore. They will pay to implement it. Bill Gates came up something that investors like and they invested in it.

Most quoted companies are ideas that the owners had little or no money but people put in their money just to be a part of the profit.

LESSON NUMBER SIXTEEN

FIND YOUR PURPOSE IN LIFE

Start early to search and locate your purpose in time. Do not be contented running on another person's track. There is a reason why God created you. There is a problem God created you to solve. Identify and solve it. Do not solve another person's problem.

LESSON NUMBER SEVENTEEN

GET ATLEAST A DEGREE FOR YOURSELF

This might not guarantee you a job or meal today but knowledge gained in attaining this level of education, if nothing, will enable you to think and reason logically as well as empower you to analyze events properly and to adequately mobilize to exploit the opportunities as they come in life.

In some countries, you are not allowed to be president of the country unless you have a first degree or its equivalent.

If you missed it early, go to night school. It is never too late to learn.

LESSON NUMBER EIGHTEEN

GO TO A SCHOOL OF MARRIAGE

Just anybody can buy a car and start to drive it with or without learning how to drive. In such a case, either the untrained driver slams into somebody or another hits him from behind.

Marriage is an important thing in life. Without it, a legal family cannot start. Without it, wholesome children cannot be produced.

Clergymen will tell you that most of the quarrels they have had to settle in the church have to do with issues of marriage and allied relationship matters. These issues have and keeps tearing marriages apart daily and by the dozen.

They say that prevention is better than cure. One way to reduce marriage crises is to study marriage and marital problems. Thank God that there are now so many Marriage Schools being set up now by certified marriage counselors to equip and send couples into marriage for better results than hitherto the case.

Attend one before getting married. It will save you so many pains.

Let me end with this simple but personal tale. When I just newly married, I had a tiff with my wife. The very first and what did I do? I left the bedroom and slept on the couch in the sitting room. The next day an elderly woman asked me where I slept and I told her. She rebuked me and advised that in future, no matter the level of disagreement, I should remain on the same bed and per chance our legs might cross and the quarrel be resolved that same night. But by going out of the bed I had only prolonged the quarrel. I kept this in mind and when I tried it, I saw effective it was.

LESSON NUMBER NINETEEN

MARRY EARLY

Forget about sowing your wild oats as some call it. Grow up responsibly. Look for a partner you will study and learn to live with and marry the person.
Stop procrastinating.
Stop giving excuses.

Stop waiting until all things are perfect.
Marry early and train your children while you are still young. Do not be caught changes nappies at seventy!

LESSON NUMBER TWEENTY

HELP YOUR CHILDREN REDEEM TIME

Set reasonable goals for your children.

Model ideals for them.

Teach them to make the best use of their time.

Help them to start and end schooling at the right time.

Make them conscious of their time and seasons.

Do not condone idleness

LESSON NUMBER TWENTY-ONE

HELP YOUR CHILDREN GET A DEGREE

Supervise their homework.

Make sure they sit all exams and give nothing but their best at all times.'

Give rewards for good performance and punish error.

Correct in love anyway.

Make them see the importance of education.

Remember that if you build houses all over the place but fail to train your children, they will not only grow up to resent you but to sell off your properties behind your back or when you are too ill to lift a finger.

LESSON NUMBER TWENTY-TWO

ESCAPE TENANCY

Nelson Mandela once said that a man is not yet a man until he has built a home.

A tenant is a slave.

Do whatever you have to do without committing a crime, to see that you have a house of your home. That saves you some rent and provides a collateral for loans when you need it.

LESSON NUMBER TWENTY-THREE

LEARN TO MIND THE COMPANY YOU KEEP

My father once told me to avoid moving with a poor man because a company is as good as the company it keeps.

The Bible says that a man who moves with fools learns

foolishness while the one moving with men of anger learns the way of anger.

They say tell me with whom you go and I will tell you what you are. Move with wise men and you will become wiser.

Move with people who know more than you because when you take what they have by way of information and add to what little you have, you will become taller than them.

A blind man cannot lead a blind man.

LESSON NUMBER TWENTY-FOUR

LEARN HOW TO MAKE MONEY

Money making is not rocket science. Find out how those who are making it are doing so.

Copy them.

You do not change a winning formula. Do not be ashamed of

investigating or going to people to ask questions. They say that a man who asks questions rarely misses the way.

The reason we have apprenticeship schemes is for people to understudy one another. Go and understudy somebody.

Nobody knows it all.

LESSON NUMBER TWENTY-FIVE

LEARN TO COMMUNICATE WELL

A closed mouth is a closed destiny. Not only must you speak out on issues that concern you, you must speak eloquently and sufficiently enough as to enable your audience comprehend what exactly you are saying.

You will not succeed in life if people have to be guessing what exactly you want or are saying. Learn how to communicate and communicate effectively. You will find later in life that this indeed is a vital tool.

LESSON NUMBER TWENTY-SIX

LEARN TO MANAGE TIME WELL

Time is the most wasting asset that you and I have. Therefore, what we do with our time matters a dozen.

Please start now to practice full utilization of your time.

Segment your activities into time zones so as to be able to make the best of the time and activities.

Work hard to see that before you are sixty, you have mastered the art of time management.

LESSON NUMBER TWENTY-SEVEN

LEARN TO SELF-BRAND

Make yourself identifiable in the market place. Do not be generic.

Make it easy for people to know what you stand for and what is special about you. if you have any skill, let the world know about it in a unique way.

If possible, fly your own flag and have a special slogan or color. For instance the South African conglomerate MTN is known with the color 'yellow'.

LESSON NUMBER TWENTY-EIGHT

LEARN TO THINK GLOBALLY

When you think globally, you see a wide market of possibilities before you.

Look into countries and find out what the comparative advantages are and capitalize on them.

Consider importation and exportation. Do not be a local champion.

God's blessing for you may be further afield.

LESSON NUMBER TWENTY-NINE

HAVE 318 SERVANTS

The Bible says that Abraham had 318 servants.

Assuming they were trained in trading, consider the amount of wealth each would be sending into the bosom of Pa Abraham.

Why not hire and train people to work for you. They will be much needed and indeed helpful when you are aging.

LESSON NUMBER THIRTY

DEVELOP FIFTY-TWO SOURCES OF INCOME

There are fifty-two weeks in a year.

If you want to run through the year without debt and hunger then develop, acquire or rent sources or ideas that can take care of the expenses of each week and leave something as savings.

LESSON NUMBER THIRTY-ONE

DEVELOP PASSIVE INCOME

When the chips are down and you can no more work, perhaps due to physical exhaustion or ill health, you need a regular source of income.

That is why you must invest in businesses and activities that can consistently generate passive income for you.

For instance, use your wealth of experience and research to write a book. Another thing you can do is shoot a film.

Hire the services of a consultant if you have to and make sure you invest in things that have long term value.

LESSON NUMBER THIRTY-TWO

LEARN TO GROW YOUR OWN FOOD

It is cheaper than buying.

You are sure that the produce are not contaminated.

They will come in handy when you do not have cash to go to the market.

Farming or gardening might be a hobby to you.

LESSON NUMBER THIRTY-THREE

HELP SIXTY PERSONS SUCCEED IN LIFE AND MINISTRY

They are seeds that you are sowing into time. The Bible says that for as long as the earth remains, seed time and harvest time will not cease.

Meaning? When you sow, you must reap. The scriptures can never be broken.

As long as you sow into people, they will surely come back to you. Learn to help others succeed. One day, they will bring the fruit of their success to you. Remember that what makes an ocean great is not the quality of its alluvial deposits. No. rather, it is the richness of the thousands of small rivers that empty into the ocean that makes it so big and blessed.

LESSON NUMBER THIRTY-FOUR

LEARN TO MAKE NOISE

Learn to blow your own trumpet. No one will blow it for you.

Let people know where you are and what you do.

It is only when people know how to reach you and what you can do for them, that they will put a demand on your anointing, skills and services.

LESSON NUMBER THIRTY-FIVE

INVEST IN TOURISM

Plan and build an event or tourist center/hotel. Or rent one instead.

Engage in activities that can drive traffic to your tourist center.

If you can, internationalize it and make the event an annual event.

Publicize and stream your event, in mass media and social media.

With time, this can become a global brand that will generate revenue even when you are asleep or too tired to work.

LESSON NUMBER THIRTY-SIX

AVOID NIGHT CLUBS

It is my personal opinion that they deny you your sleep.

The noise level is toxic.

It is often a den of questionable characters.

Second hand smoking is a possibility.
 You might stumble into a strip tease someday, in the process of patronize night clubs.

This is not a business advice but I am convinced you can get better relaxation elsewhere.

LESSON NUMBER THIRTY-SEVEN

LEARN TO MANAGE YOUR HEALTH

Visit your doctor even when you think you are health. Go for regular checkups.

Avoid self-medication and over-doses.

Exercise regularly.

LESSON NUMBER THIRTY-EIGHT

LEARN TO EAT YOUR FOOD AS MEDICINE

Do not eat to please your eyes only. Do not eat because your nose like the food. Do not eat because your ego likes the environment. Do not eat because the meal is pocket friendly.
Eat because the meal has nutritional value. Eat because of the medicinal value. Eat because it can digest easily. Eat because all said and done, the meal will boost your health. No more, no less.

LESSON NUMBER THIRTY-NINE

RUN INTEGRATED BUSINESSES

Aim at having zero waste in your business and let one aspect of your business, feed the other.

Learn to integrate forward, backward and sideways if possible.

Let me give you an example. You are a business man running a chain of eateries. Definitely, you need to integrate forward into supplying the food to those in offices and distant places as opposed to selling only to people who come to the traditional place of sale.

You also want to own farms to ensure supply of raw materials for your meals as well as go into packaging to make sure that the farm produce reach your kitchen in good shape and also supply other members of the public who may be in need of raw food.

LESSON NUMBER FORTY

VISIT A PRISON YARD

When in-mates tell you what brought them into prison you will be shocked. Some of the offences were things you were taking for

granted but which has sent somebody else to jail.
That makes us more careful and mindful on how we relate with others.

When we venture to the condemned criminals' side, we discover that most of them killed others due to lack of self-control.

This makes us in turn to practice self-control.

Some are there because they moved with the wrong people or were apprehended at the wrong place.

From this also, we learn that we should mind whom we moved with and places to avoid completely.

LESSON NUMBER
FORTYONE

VISIT AN AUTOPAEDIC HOSPITAL

We must learn to be grateful to God in all we do.

One way to learn the magnitude of what God is doing for us is to visit the hospitals. There you will see people whose limbs are broken and those breathing only with the aid of machines. You see people with all manners of sickness and who have almost lost all hopes of ever leaving the hospital. There you meet with many with incurable diseases and they are in isolation despite the millions that they have in the bank.

This teaches us humility and contentment. We should be grateful to God for waking us up each day. If you think that it is the alarm clock, as I have heard people say, that wakes us up, buy and alarm clock and set it before the dead and see whether they will wake up.

Make it a habit to visit hospitals because it will help sharpen your appreciation of God and all that he is doing for you.

LESSON NUMBER FORTY-TWO

LEARN TO WORK FROM HOME

Whether you like it or not, a time comes in the life of every person when we can no more go out on a daily basis to where ever we call or tag office – we just have to learn how to work from home.

Some of us are so fixated and used to the idea of an office that any other place makes us sick.

My advice is start early to learn how to work from home.

Right now fortunately, most businesses are done online. That means that fortunes are being made using computers and handsets as well as social media. People do not have to leave their homes to hit millions these days.

We must start early to adapt ourselves to this reality.

LESSON NUMBER FORTY-THREE

LIVE IN LAGOS AT LEAST FOR SEVEN YEARS

It has been said that Lagos with over twenty million residents, is a university of its own.
There are many lessons that Lagos can teach a man and does teach people every day. If a person can survive in Lagos for seven years,

he can survive anywhere in the world.

LESSON NUMBER FORTY-FOUR

LEARN TO SAY NO TO ALCOHOL

The Bible says give wine to those who are perishing.

I say drink wine if you want to perish.

You cannot drink and drive because the alcohol will dull your senses. You cannot drink and operate machines for the same reason.

Now that you are still young, you must learn to avoid alcohol because when you get older and you cannot even stand without the support of a walking stick, alcohol in your system will just be like a wicked man by your side pushing you to fall unto an on-coming train or into a ditch you would have seen and recognized without the effect of alcohol.

Practice early to do without alcohol because a dog does not learn how to be left handed in old age.

Alcohol destroys your scruples bringing to the same level as the city without walls and which cannot stop anything from entering.

LESSON NUMBER FORTY-FIVE

LEARN TO SAY THANK YOU

When you thank a man for what he has done, he will have the strength to do more.

Learn to say thank you even when you are insulted. It is a magic word that douses tension.

Thank you, said with passion, wins a friend always. Learn to use it to open doors of opportunity in life.

LESSON NUMBER FORTY-SIX

LEARN TO SAY NO TO GAMBLING

Imagine what life will be like if you should lose all your gratuity to a roll of the dice or a jump by a race horse.

Many a homeless senior citizen was sent to the streets or sleeping under the city bridges by a demon called Gambling.

It is a demon we must not eat at all with, not to talk of a long spoon, if we want to enjoy our old age in peace and without regrets.

I have seen a man lose his fortune in just one stake.

LESSON NUMBER FORTY-SEVEN

LEARN TO SAY NO TO MULTIPLE WIVES

With no insult intended, I agree with those who say one woman one trouble.

A man who multiplies his wives have multiplied his troubles.

Even when the new wife is coming to you without cost, there are always some long run costs and hidden charges!

For instance, more wives mean more in-laws to relate with.

LESSON FORTY-EIGHT

LEARN HOW TO SMILE

Permit me to quote the lyrics of the Rotary Club song which says:

"Smile everyone, smile.

Smile and your troubles will vanish like bubbles;

Smile everyone, smile."

Learn to smile even in the face of great adversity.

LESSON NUMBER FORTY-NINE

BE SOMEBODY'S APPRENTICE

Look for somebody who is doing well in life and business.

When you have found such a person, do not let pride or what people would say hold you back. Go and meet the person ask to be accepted as an apprentice.

You do not change a winning formula instead, you copy it.

LESSON NUMBER FIFTY

LEARN HOW TO REST

All works and no play makes jack a dull boy.

The Bible tells me that even God Almighty rested after creation. We must learn to rest no matter how relevant we think we are.

If we should fall sick, we will be taken to hospital and we are given what they call 'bed rest' which in my opinion is nothing but compulsory rest.

We should know that many squander their health looking for wealth, so much so that when eventually they have the material wealth, they lack the health to enjoy the wealth. That is why today we have so many rich men who have food but cannot eat.

A vital thing to learn and master before age sixty is to relax at given intervals and rest.

A Nigerian proverb says that the hunter who misses his sleep time, might get to the land of the dead before his prey.

LESSON NUMBER FIFTY-ONE

LEARN WHEN TO COUNT YOUR MONEY

Avoid premature celebration. Wait until every deal is sealed and done before spending.

Do not count your chicks before they are hatched.

LESSON NUMBER FIFTY-TWO

OWN A CITY

This looks tough but that is what faith can do. If you have a dream that your calculation can start and finish, then there is nothing divine about it. Ask God for a miracle.

Dream big and aim high. Start now to work towards owning a city. Some may choose to call it an estate. Well that is a matter of nomenclature.

When you own the estate or city of your own, you will be in control of certain things like the shops, schools, water supply, security system, hospital, etc. that will feed your unborn generation. Others may buy and own the buildings but the utilities belong to you. This could be one of your strategic investments.

LESSON NUMBER FIFTY-THREE

TRY AND UNDERSTAND SHARE CROPPING

You will need this as you age with particular regard to food production.

This is an arrangement in which you provide farm tools and seeds to others who go to the farm and labor and at the end of the harvest season, the yield of the farm is shared among the partners.

This is good for you because it is not energy sapping. This work well when the partners can be trusted. Enter into written agreement with them if possible.

LESSON NUMBER FIFTY-FOUR

TRY AND UNDERSTAND NETWORKING

Learn to network. Learn to sell things via network marketing. In the world we are in today, almost everything, from food supplements to cars and other vehicles, are being sold via network marketing.

To live without knowing anything or enough on network marketing is like the ostrich burying its head in the ground and assuming that will take care of the enemy.

LESSON NUMBER FIFTY-FIVE

NEVER RETIRE

Tiredness is in the mind. Tell yourself always that you have not done enough. Re-fire and re-activate your zeal to serve.

As long as a man is active and alive, he should never give up on life or himself.

Teach yourself how to be self-motivating. Learn how to encourage yourself in the Lord. Start now to learn it so that when the chips are down, you will be able to pick up the pieces at any time.

For instance, when those you are working for or with think that you are milked and dry, develop the capacity and capability to show them that you still got some millage to go.

LESSON NUMBER FIFTY-SIX

ENDOW YOUR CHILDREN

These days, it is not enough to train your children. Even with the very best grades possible from the very best of institutions, there are still no jobs for the youths.
It appears that the only way forward is that each youth must

carve a niche for his or herself and go into business and they cannot do this without adequate capital. One way to help is to save and work towards leaving some capital for your children to enable them launch into the world of business on a solid and not slippery note.

LESSON NUMBER FIFTY-SEVEN

THINK FOR OTHERS

Be a mentor to others. This has to do more with your peers. Mix and encourage one another. Like you, their children must have gone out of the nest in search of life and what it has to offer. Thus leaving them alone in big and expansive houses. Stand in gap for one another.

Do not retreat into your shell.

Be a role model for others. Let them come to you for leadership by example.

Let them come to you for counseling. Make out time for others.

Do not retire into a high fence.

LESSON NUMBER FIFTY-EIGHT

SET UP TEACHING OPPORTUNITIES

Now that you are close to retirement or have already retired, do well to set up teaching engagements. You can volunteer to teach in schools as a way of keeping busy.

Share your knowledge and experience with the younger generation. Do not allow experience to be their teacher because sometimes, experience can be very expensive.

They will not only be grateful, it will help make the world a better place for all of mankind.

LESSON NUMBER FIFTY-NINE

JOIN THE ARMY OR PARA MILITARY

Doing this on part time will bring more discipline and exercise into our life. It is one sure way of fighting boredom. It will help you fight off idleness which kills a lot of retirees before their time.

LESSON NUMBER SIXTY

ACQUIRE COMPUTER KNOWLEDGE

We are in a knowledge based age. The world today is technology driven AND UNLESS one is technology savvy, there is a great possibility of being left behind.

Whatever it takes, one should work hard to learn today's language which is Technology. Robots and intelligent or smart houses are built around technology. Therefore in your getting, get artificial intelligence and sell it not.

The End.

BOOKS BY THE SAME AUTHOR

1. Why A Christian Should Not Be Called Augustine.
2. How to Know a Mad Pastor.
3. 14 Surprising Things We Do That Put People Off Christianity.
4. Why Many Pastors Preach Beyond Allotted Time.

6. How to Pray Against Terrorism.

7. Hundred Things a Pastor Can Do To Help Government

8. 77 Benefits of Foreign Missions.

9. How to Increase Your Ministerial Connections.

1. Hundred Bad Thing Members Do To Their Pastors.

2. PARENTING: Twenty Surprising Things A Lousy Woman Can Never Tell Her Daughter.

3. How A Christian Can Receive Cash Daily.

4. One Hundred And Ten Prayer Points for Married Women.

5. Something Worse Than Witchcraft.

6. Twenty-one Irrefutable Ways Pastors Expose Themselves To Sexual Immorality.

7. Forty Prayer Points for Tithe Payers.

8. Why Telephone Counseling?

9. GRIEF MANAGEMENT: What to Say when Everyone Else is crying.

10. LONGEVITY: What My Grandfather Did To Reach

One Hundred and Twenty Years.

11.   Seven Deadly Things That Should Never Happen To A Christian.

12.   One Serious Spiritual Mistake the United States of America is making.

13.   Forty Time Thieves.

14.   More Benefits of Online Education

15.   How To Make People Work for You While Calling You A Fool.

16.   Twenty One Ways Christians Become Cursed Without Knowing.

17. What Really Happened To Biblical Fasting?
18. So You Call Yourself A Manager?

19. APOSTASY: How One can Fall into It Without Knowing.

20. FORTY PRAYER POINTS AGAINST RISING AND FALING.

21. WHY I WAS ARRESTED IN TOGO

22. HOW TO SELL THE SEEMINGLY UNSELLABLE

23. FIVE SECRETS MY FATHER REVEALED TO ME IN 1975

YOU MADE A WISE DECISION!

What makes us so confident in making the above assertion?

It is certainly not because the author:

BISHOP O. INNOCENT

is the president of a seminary and a pastor of many years standing. No!

One word from God through this book is enough to lift your destiny!

Remember that God spoke through a Donkey in the Bible. He can use anyone or book to speak to you.

May the Lord bring this to pass in your life, in Jesus name, we pray!

THANK YOU

- For making out time to read this book. The author will appreciate your honest comments for the improvement of this book in subsequent editions.

For that purpose, kindly contact the author on:

Email: newochei@gmail.com

Thanks and God bless you.

ABOUT THE AUTHOR

Before giving his life to Jesus Christ in a Reinhardt Bornke Crusade in Lagos, Nigeria, Bishop O. Innocent was the Managing Editor of **Katsina Newsweek**. He was not only involved in managing the organization, he had the responsibility of polishing young journalist in the art of reporting, news subbing and editing.

He later became drafted by Zoe Ministries Worldwide a ministry with over 10,000 man congregation at one of its branches and over a thousand branches worldwide including but not limited to UK and USA; to manage her media outfit which he did from 1992 to 1995.

Bishop O. Innocent attended various higher institutions and got admitted as a member of the **Institute of Management Consultants,** amongst others.

He started a congregation in 1996. But despite his practical experience in Zoe Ministries, bible school and his skills as a manger, he still struggled. This forced him to take deep interest in the counsel of Apostle Paul to Timothy to study to show thyself approved.

In addition to going back to Bible School for higher studies, Bishop O. Innocent took great interest in studying the dynamics of Ministry. Though he occasionally teaches other subjects such as Prayer Life and Deliverance, that are in sync with ministry, he made **MINISTRY**, the main object of his study.

Little did he know that God was calling him to a deeper, life-long teaching ministry! As a young enthusiastic church planter, he planted seven churches within two years and was almost carried away until one faithful day.
The Lord sent a prophet to him while he was in company of three others (two still alive) and said to him:

"Though what you do now as a pastor is necessary, I have called you to go out and strengthen pastors as a teacher".

With further explanation, Bishop Ochei understood and after much prayers, he began an outreach ministry premised on joint seminars with various ministerial associations and fellowships: such at the Pentecostal Fellowship of Nigeria chapters mainly in and around Abuja (Gwagwalada, IDU, DEIDEI, KAURU,

NYANYA, MASSIKA, and MARARABA) Niger State (Suleija, Madaka, Rafinsenyi, etc) and in the west and mid-western states. The Lord has also taken him to several major cities across eastern Nigeria.

With time, the Lord opened the doors of foreign missions and Bishop O. Innocent found himself teaching and explaining MINISTRY to the extent he understood it to ministers in Liberia, Ghana, Togo, Cameroun, Corte d'lvoire, Burkina Faso, Sierra Leone, Guinea and in contact with ministers from USA, Holland, Australia, India, Pakistan etc. with whom he partnered to spread the teaching of Ministry. It would be an understatement to say that he has directly reached over ten thousand ministers of the gospel and still counting.

The aim above is not to name drop. Rather, it must be emphasized that these diversified audiences, kept him on his toes by most times asking him questions for some of which he did not have answer! Thus, forcing him to run back to more study and consultation with the Holy Spirit our biggest teacher.

His own nuclear family has been a major force in his quest for knowledge of things of God. His last born child of four is [now as 18) 300-level University student, while the rest have graduated and are in Christ. They most times ask questions that make Bishop O. Innocent, more often than not, go extra mile in preparing for the family devotion at 10:00pm every day.

For instance one day, Benita asked:
"Dad is it true that God eats our praises?"
'Yes' he replied.
"Then after "eating" praises what does God drink?" the young girl asked.
Bishop O. Innocent wondered what one word he would have given in answer to the question. So when he got to the next port of teaching, he put the question to the ministers present. The one –word

answers were as many as there were ministers!

Sometimes the ministers themselves box Bishop Ochei to the corner. When Rev. Able Kpanke was still the PFN Chairman in Gwagwalada, Abuja, about fifteen years ago, at the end a five day School of Ministry, ministers, in the course of giving a vote of thanks, one of the pastors asked Bishop O. Innocent: ***"What is your take on Cloning and GMO Food now in circulation in Africa and what should be the position of the church on this?"***

Believe me, that was the first time of Bishop O. Innocent hearing the two words ***"Cloning and Genetically Modified Organisms"*** Though the Holy Spirit helped him say something acceptable and a new date was fixed for an extensive discussion of the issue, such encounters have spurred the bishop to burn more midnight candle.

The above encounter with the Pastors in Gwagwalada, Abuja bore fruit in some years later, as the PFN, Asaba Delta State Nigeria (under Rev. Duke of Church of God Mission at the time) invited him and he gave a talk on ***"Hundred Latest Development in the World and How they Affect the Church"***

What this means is that whatever a teacher knows is often, precipitated by the interest of his listeners! To that extent we dare say that Bishop O. Innocent as a teacher is the by-product of much in-put of the pastors and other clergy he has been privileged to minister to in the course of his twenty-five years of teaching!

He has also been influenced by the several seminars and conferences he has attended, as well as the teaching of so many great teachers he has sat under including but not limited to Paul Olson, author of ***"How to Heal A leper"*** and Late founder of New Day Ministries,

Mound, Minnesota, USA Rev. Damaris Faulkner of International Fellowship of Christian Crisis Centers, USA, Dr. Ron Spoelma and Dr. Bob Meyer of Holy Passion Church, Almere, Holland, etc. He continues to learn by reading at least forty books on any topic before he teaches on it and he reads at least one book a week.

As at the time of writing this book, he has about seventy (70) books online in addition to about twenty other hard copy books published locally in Nigeria on various subjects.

Happily married to Rev. (Prophetess) Mrs. Lizzy, an Assistant Director of Education in Lagos State, Nigeria and founding Senior Pastor of Miracle Arena Ministries, Lagos, Nigeria, Bishop O. Innocent is currently the President, New Day Ministerial Association and New Day College of Bishop which are fellowships of all pastors and bishops trained and ordained by Paul Olson, in Africa before he went to be with the

Lord as well as those who love the vision which is simply ***to identify possible barriers and hindrances capable of stopping a minister from preaching the gospel and doing all humanly possible to remove them.***

Bishop O. Innocent is also the current President of New Dimension Seminaries International, which has students in several nations.
He can be reached on:
Email: newochei@gmail.com   Tel: +234 80345530436

NOTES

NOTES

www.ingramcontent.com/pod-product-compliance
Lightning Source LLC
Chambersburg PA
CBHW031419210526
45464CB00005B/1961